Planets

by Martha E. H. Rustad

Raintree is an imprint of Capstone Global Library Limited, a company incorporated in England and Wales having its registered office at 264 Banbury Road, Oxford, OX2 7DY – Registered company number: 6695582

www.raintree.co.uk
myorders@raintree.co.uk

Edited by Erika L. Shores
Designed by Juliette Peters and Katelin Plekkenpol
Picture research by Tracy Cummins
Production by Katy LaVigne
Originated by Capstone Global Library

Printed and bound in China.

ISBN 978 1 4747 1250 7 (hardback)

19 18 17 16 15
10 9 8 7 6 5 4 3 2 1

ISBN 978 1 4747 1254 5 (paperback)

20 19 18 17 16
10 9 8 7 6 5 4 3 2 1

British Library Cataloguing in Publication Data
A full catalogue record for this book is available from the British Library.

Acknowledgements
We would like to thank the following for permission to reproduce photographs: NASA: JPL, 17; Science Source: SPL, 11, 21; Shutterstock: cigdem, 15, Kalenik Hanna, Design Element, manjik, 9, Michelangelus, 7, Tristan3D, 19, Vadim Sadovski, 13, Thinkstock: rwarnick, cover, 1; Wikimedia: NASA/ GSFC/NOAA/USGS, 5.

Every effort has been made to contact copyright holders of material reproduced in this book. Any omissions will be rectified in subsequent printings if notice is given to the publisher.

Editor's Note
In this book's photographs, the sizes of objects and the distances between them are not to scale.

Contents

Home, sweet home!

We live on Earth.

It is a planet.

Planets orbit stars.

The Sun is a star.

7

The Sun has eight planets.

Earth is one of them.

Close to the Sun

Mercury and Venus are
close to the Sun.
Mars and Earth are, too.

Mercury

Venus

Earth

Mars

They are called

the inner planets.

They are made of rock.

Mercury

Far away

Jupiter and Saturn are far
from the Sun.

Uranus and Neptune are, too.

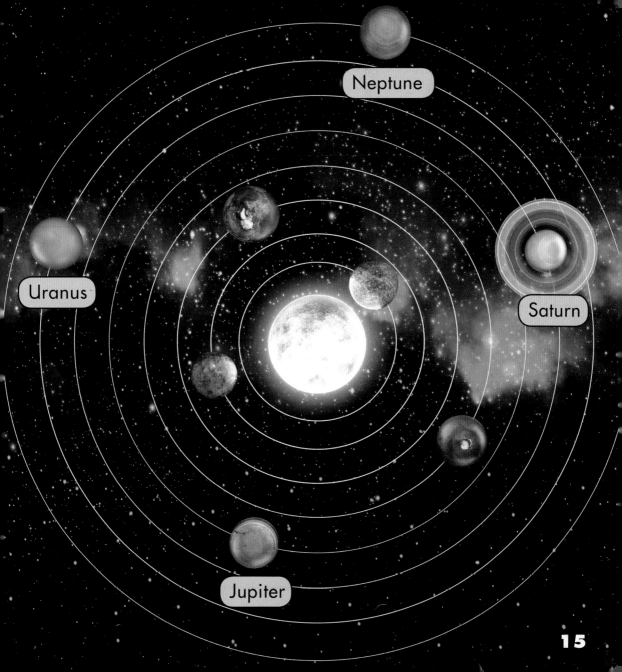

Neptune

Uranus

Saturn

Jupiter

They are called
the outer planets.
They are made of gas.

Neptune

Uranus

Saturn

Jupiter

The outer planets are big.

Jupiter is as big as

1,300 Earths.

Earth

Jupiter

Look up. See the night sky.

You can spot some planets!

Saturn

Mars

Venus

Mercury

Glossary

gas substance that spreads to fill any space that holds it

orbit follow a curved path around an object in space

planet large object in space that orbits a star

star ball of burning gases

Find out more

Little Kid's First Big Book of Space, Catherine D. Hughes (National Geographic, 2012)

Planets (Space), Charlotte Guillain (Raintree, 2010)

Websites

solarsystem.nasa.gov/planets/whatisaplanet.cfm
Visit this website to learn about planets.

www.bbc.co.uk/education/topics/zdbbkqt
Watch videos about the solar system on this website.

Index